"WOUNDED SOULS"

A COLLECTION OF POEMS AND SONGS
BY INGRID D. JOHNSON

iUniverse, Inc.
New York   Bloomington

iUniverse books may be ordered through booksellers or by contacting:

iUniverse
1663 Liberty Drive
Bloomington, IN 47403
www.iuniverse.com
1-800-Authors (1-800-288-4677)

ISBN: 978-1-4401-6597-9 (sc)
ISBN: 978-1-4401-6604-4 (dj)
ISBN: 978-1-4401-6598-6 (ebook)

Printed in the United States of America

iUniverse rev. date:08/31/2009

DEDICATIONS

I dedicate this book to God,
His son Jesus Christ, and The Holy spirit
who never ceases to amaze me.

To my close friends & my family,
whom I love unconditionally.
Thank you for believing in me.

To Catherine Hudek thank you for
introducing me to the power of poems.
Everything you did helped me.

To my late grandmother, my great-grandmother,
and Don G. ... you will always be in my heart, R.I.P.

To all the poets, writers, musicians,
motivational speakers, preachers, prophets,
ministers, spoken word artist, slam poets, and
independent film makers who inspire me
to write, sing, do spoken word, and reach
for my dreams this ones for you.

To: Billie Holiday, Etta James, Sarah Vaughn,
Ella Fitzgerald, Sade, Tina Turner, Jill Scott, Deepa Mehta,
Alice Walker, Toni Morrison, Robert Collier,
Beverly Engel, Linda Schierse Lenoard,
Jim Morrison, Jonetta Rose Barras, Francine Rivers,
John Powell, Akosua Busia, Regina Louise,
Jan Stiller Gaopelle, Tori Amos, The Roots,
Talib Kwe'li, Outkast, Erykah Badu, Mos Def,
Nas, Alicia Keys, Floetry, Bjork, Estelle,
Lauryn Hill, KOS, Damien and Stephen Marley.
Thank you for inspiring me to keep on putting
pen to paper, my nose to the grind stone,

my lips to the mic, and hands together in prayer
to ask God (through Jesus Christ) for more creativity, boldness
and courage in sharing the peaceful,
intensity, of my every day life.

"... But he was pierced for our offenses, crushed for our sins, upon him was the chastisement that makes us whole, by his stripes we were healed."

- ISAIAH 53:5-

This book is dedicated to Wounded Souls everywhere
struggling to learn
struggling to rise
struggling to heal
AND
ready for change - ready to love
I feel you
and with God
we shall all overcome!

Contents

IN THE CLOSET PRODUCTIONS

FOREWORD

Poetry has always represented a medium for truth, introspection, and an outlet of creative expression to me. It is the mirror that allows me to see myself and the rest of the world clearly. It is one of my most cherished gifts from God above and the one place where I can bravely confront the demons trying to torment me with the past.

After the release of "Little Black Butterfly in Iridescent Sunlight," on July.13th 2005, I received a lot of wonderful opportunities to promote my book. These opportunities came through The Metro and the Lance community paper, Uptown Magazine, and The Winnipeg Public Library newsletter. In addition to interviews on CBC national news, CBC radio one, CBC local news and CBC news world, CKUW"s "Grammar Skool", "Say it Sista", and "What a Feminist sounds like," Shaw T.V., Hot 103, UMFM radio, Café 100.7, Winnipeg's Flava 107.9, and Bravo! News. I was very surprised and I never expected Winnipeg to be so supportive or to see my book become number 5 on McNally Robinson's bestsellers list. Months later, I was blessed with the gift of songwriting and on November 2nd , 2007 I celebrated the release of my first 8 songwriting efforts on local Winnipeg artist Flo's, self-titled debut album titled "FLO" that The Winnipeg Free Press and The Winnipeg Sun rated 4 out of 5 stars. All of these experiences gave me "butterflies" and solidified my purpose, I was born to write, speak, and sing God's truth with love, into other people's lives.

At twenty-eight, through God, I had managed to take all my years filled with low self-esteem, depression, heartbreak, rage, and traumatic childhood memories of sexual abuse and turn them into what some would say, a dream come true. I was shocked by this reality and although everything seem to be coming up roses in my world, inside I still felt like a very lost and sad little girl. I was still at war with myself and filled with a fear, rage, mistrust, sadness, and endless confusion. I needed and wanted to change. I didn't want to feel like a victim or a survivor any longer. I wanted to feel like more than a conqueror. I wanted to experience more miracles and more wonderful blessings in my life. I wanted my words to change people's lives for the better, but most of all I wanted to be "a voice for the voiceless" children in the world, destroyed by abuse and filled with self-hate. They needed someone to speak up for them and share their stories with the world. I wanted to create a successful music, publishing, and production company ("In The Closet Productions") that would help to bring awareness to overcoming the emotional, spiritual, mental, and physical trauma of sexual abuse, through various works of art.

In August 2006, I set out to establish my independent music publishing, book publishing, film, and show production company. Then, I waved goodbye to mourning my childhood, stepped into my womanhood, and found all sorts of people and obstacles that opposed my new sense of self and my new found vision and dream. These people hated my voice and I was surprised to be called all sort of names and accused of all sort of things just for educating myself, being organized, business like, and respectful in the industry. They hated that I was in touch with my core and aware of falsehood and corrupt character traits. They hated that I refused to be manipulated and guilt tripped into accepting responsibility for their negative actions but it didn't matter because God was on my side.

Over the course of 3 1/2 years I was shocked by the reasons some people used to stop being my friend. They didn't like the new person I had become. They despised my new found relationship with God and the wisdom I found in knowing Jesus Christ, so they tried to make me doubt myself but their efforts only made me grow wiser, bolder, more loving, full of faith, and stronger in God.

This second collection of poetry is an spiritual, physical, mental, and emotional journey into places filled with doubt, fear, confusion, questions, old wounds, hope, new beginnings, and most of all love, peace, and JOY. It is my transition from being a woman that worshipped people more than God and who wrote with a poison pen until I found myself, no longer broken in His arms. It is a book filled with snapshots from my continuous journey towards change, inner peace, and most of all, true unconditional LOVE. I hope it brings you wisdom, truth, light, understanding, comfort, and peace ... wherever you are in your life. Thank you and may God bless you for supporting this new body of work.

LITTLE EARTH QUAKES

MY TESTIMONY

Do you know what it's like
to be quiet
to be numb
to be still
I mean
for a really long time
to disappear into
relationship after
relationship
not really sharing
your opinions, your feelings,
your heart, your thoughts
until you are mute
and function more like
a phantom
wearing no mask
but still hidden inside
the horror of your past
Do you know what
its like to be incomplete

Do you know what it is like
To always run across buildings
in your dreams
hoping one day you will fall and fly
Away from the truth that pursues you
and your lies …daily
the lies that leave you
scared and scarred …
and your TRUST
assassinated in the dark
so long time ago
when your boogie man
pulled you in the closet

and shut off all the lights
in that white little house with
the dark chocolate trim
on Maryland Street
still standing so neat after 29 years

Do you know what its like
when your world is bigger
on the inside
and always dark all around you
when you are haunted by a cloud
that wants to depress you with memories
huddled over that toilet bowl
next to the pearly white sink
puking out your soul
with him hanging next to you
and you too innocent and naive to scream
but wise enough to dream your way
out of a really uncomfortable scene
for years
quietly muffling your butterflies
and crushing your wings
until one day everything is triggered
and images flash full screen
across your mind
leaving you trapped in time
and nervous
riding on the number 17
next to the old man gumming his food
like that demon - use to gum you
in eerie silence
before all the lights
would go out in the room
29 years ago
before you could whisper this to yourself
You don't own me anymore
It was your sin and it was never my fault

So you no longer define me
I can be whatever I want
Most of all I am free to speak
So, no more running after illusions
no more paying attention to them in the dark
you will not spoon feed me lies anymore
and force me to keep everything you did inside
because I was made in my daddy's image
fearfully and wonderfully made
A princess - a Queen
Able to shine without spotlights
Able to produce my own dreams
refusing to let anyone make choices for me
Out in this classroom … called life
Where last month I learned to scream
Last week I learned to shout
Yesterday I learned to use and project
My unique singing voice
to touch them the way love does - deeply
and God willing the way Billie Holiday's blues
did reducing them to tears
("Them that's Got shall get …
Them that's not shall lose…
so the Bible says and it still is news …")
And today
Yes, today of all days
I am learning how to stop
and breathe in the life of God
so I can spit out … some of God's
uncensored truth to you …
if you are lonely, if you are silent,
if you are broken, if you are wounded,
if you are in need of healing deep down
on the inside where most humans
are bleeding … to death
Seek God's Kingdom and know that life, Wisdom, truth
peace, Joy, understanding, forgiveness and true

unconditional love … shall be yours
and abundantly added unto you
forever and ever and ever and ever and ever
AMEN

This is my testimony
My life will be the proof
That I can do more than just survive
Pain, depression, rejection
and my childhood riddled with
verbal, emotional, physical, spiritual,
psychological, and sexual abuse
now that I have the God's truth

MISSED DIAGNOSED (For LISA)

They say
She will never learn
to trust
that sexual abuse is a disease
like CANCER
that will continue
to destroy her soul
over and over again
so we should all just let her be
comfortable being uncomfortable
instead of trying to set her free

"We can't change her" … they say
As they jot down her problems
reasons why She will never succeed
in the years ahead
Categorizing them - one by one
on lined paper in 4 little steps
until they lock her up
in a broken system
a lonely dirty prison
reminiscent of residential schools
where aboriginal children
were never free to leave

But she is only eight
Yet in their ignorance
they think they have her
all figured out
and bereft of all hope
they pollute the room with doubt
so proud of the diagnosis that was made
they crown themselves experts in their field
unaware of how she hurts and truly feels

cause their so certain that her path
will be a road riddled with mistrust, failure,
dysfunction, and out of wedlock pregnancies

In the morning
they gossip about her situation
while I fume with explosive agitation
about their disinterest in any real solutions
that disputes their confirmation
about their lack of faith in her adult recovery
so with all sorts of allegations
they prophecy a life for her
filled with endless years of tragedy

But I say – I say
All children are God's property
and all adults are responsible
for guiding them to a positive outcome
and I say all children at any age
can heal
A child at any age can learn
to trust again
to search for God and find
their true purpose in Him
A child can learn to recognize
and speak the truth again
A child can learn to love and regain
what was taken
A child can learn to live by listening
To God's gentle still voice from deep within
A dysfunctional child can CHANGE
and be made pure and innocent again
Because I was like her too
Unable to trust and always ready to lie
out of fear of being hurt and rejected again
A child destroyed by LUST not LOVE
Until I learned to spread my wings

and give what I received from God
and some people who
took the time to teach me
TRUE UNCONDITIONAL LOVE
God's truth and all His promises for me
through His son Jesus Christ who
died on a cross for me

But they don't want to hear about that
Or believe that His existence
Truly can set her soul free
Because He is hidden and unseen
and requires an open heart
and a child's imagination
in order to restore
worlds filled with pain
and endless devastation

SURVIVORS CHANT

I was drowning in Emotion
when You sent peace to my Ocean

(and they tried to separate us)

Eighteen years incarceration
My soul craved for elevation

(and they tried to destroy us)

And,
I don't know
I don't know
I don't know
I don't know …
what they think they can do here

Like the Wise men in the Bible
You gave me skills for my survival

(and they tried to destroy us)

And,
I don't know
I don't know
I don't know
I don't know …
what they think they can do here

Cause, this soul is a survivor
and You blessed me to be
Your writer

So,
I don't know
I don't know
I don't know
I don't know …
what they think they can do here

As a child You spoke to me
through all my visions and my dreams

So,
I don't know
I don't know
I don't know
I don't know …
what they think they can do here

And when the enemy arrived
And tried to take my life

(He couldn't separate us)

So,
I don't know
I don't know
I don't know
I don't know …
what they think they can do here

You picked me up when I was down
and rose me to Your higher ground

So,
Yes, I'm sure
Yes, I'm sure

Yes, I'm sure
Yes, I'm sure …
that there is nothing they can do here

I thank you for the son you gave
I sing your glory and give You praise

So,
Yes, I'm sure
Yes, I'm sure
Yes, I'm sure
Yes, I'm sure …
that there is nothing they can do here

I thank you for my self-esteem
You're the inspiration
for all my dreams

(and I know that they will come true)

Cause,
Yes, I'm sure
Yes, I'm sure
Yes, I'm sure
Yes, I'm sure
Yes, I'm sure
Yes, I'm sure
Yes, I'm sure …
Yes, I'm sure

that You will never leave me

THE BOOGIE MAN

I remember
the violence
the tears
that bubbled
and backed up
inside your throat
when you spoke of him
when you asked
if I could come
and get you at 1 a.m.
because he had
lost it again
and held a knife
to your throat
for talking back to him

I remember how
defenseless I felt
hearing your muffled cries
through the telephone
knowing that you
were traumatized
and all alone
destroyed by his
malicious
attempt to silence you

He was such a monster
but you loved him
anyway
and I wanted to
become an overnight
assassin and take
vengeance in your name

but there was nothing
that I could do
even though he was
manipulating you
terrorizing you
and I wanted so badly
to protect you and
take you away from him
so that he couldn't
hurt you again
but my spirit was
too weak
to speak up for you
and your little boy
who was only two
because I had
no resources
and even less knowledge
on how to save you
from the boogie man
inside of your closet

THE FUNERAL

She lay silent
 with grief stricken
   relatives
exhaling accolades
over the pungent
     smell
of her
corrosive limbs
dressed in white linen
poised in a custom made
         crib
 designed for the dead
 as I clung to our final
 memories of intimacy
   weeping profusely
in front of a television screen
   instead of a cemetery
Wondering if I will ever
     see her again

THE WARRIOR
(For my Late Grandmother Addassa)

ssshhhh …listen
can you hear that
people are coming
people are screaming
and the ambulance
is running
and crying out for me
But I'm not ready yet
So this is all
just a dream to me
a false prophecy
confirmed by this I.V.
and the tiny drops
of morphine
itching my skin
I can still feel everything

Now a nurse with
white hair
gives me a shot of insulin
and I know that they
all think
it's all over for me
I can see it on their faces
But
this battle is just the beginning
and they don't know everything
about the series of wars
that I've been in
because they only have
50% of the equation
to solve this problem
that they call a disease

and the other half lies
in my state of being
and my will for self-preservation
and although
I am struggling to stay alive
I know it's not time
to go yet to the other side

Cause
I'm not finished yet
and my body is a temple
that my soul refuses
to leave
that's why I'm stronger than
this Cancerous disease
that is trying to destroy
my body systematically

Look at them
Starring at me
surrounding me
waiting for me
to accept their prognosis
But this is just another test
and they have no
divine providence
So, I'm not ready yet
Because there's just too much
to do
too much to see
like my younger daughter's
wedding
and my grand daughter's
first book

she's turned into quite
the little butterfly
with the power to hook
anyone willing to listen
to her words
So
I'm not going anywhere
until she explodes
into something big
I still got some more
life to live

So
go on run your bone marrow
test
and radiation treatments
and when it's all over
I'll still be living
And not that
Cancerous demon
because my soul is
eternal
nocturnal
and there are people
counting on me
to keep my promises
So
I'll go out
on my own terms
on a day that I
choose
Until then
I'll take your pills
with some spiritual food
and then let my God
do his work

Because
the cure isn't out there
it's already here
inside of me – it's in my nature
that has the cure for any
mortal disease
just ask her
she knows
she sees
the answers are
in her plants and trees
and the manual for my body
is with God
that's why I can still breathe
10 years past the time
you diagnosed me
with this horrible disease
So your concerns
never traumatized me
they just allowed me
to savor every minute
every hour of every single day
So that I could
plant kisses all over
my brand new grandson's face
and create new memories
with my eldest daughter
that time cannot erase

I've gone back home
several times
and sat and laughed
with all of my sisters
and generations
after me
So my house
is in order

and if death
is my final destiny
I'll embrace it
willingly
when it comes
knowing it is only
a promotion
into a new state
of being
where I will get to
watch over
those I love
as they celebrate
my memory
and the battles
I've won on Earth
and now over stand
in Heaven
So
When you get
lonely for me
close your eyes
and look for me
and you will see me
forever dancing –dancing
in your dreams

PRODIGAL DAUGHTER

I am trying
so hard
to understand you Mother
but you are
an enigma to me
the enigma within me
that won't let me be
showing your love
in such abstract ways
that makes me wonder
why God gave me to you at birth
when we are so different
but yet so much the same
two strong women
screaming at the very same dream
to be loved
to be loved
to be loved
oh, to be loved
and also to be respected

THE DEAD MAN'S CHAIR

Looking at the dead man's chair
we debate about money
not being the root of all evil
but man's love of it in a material world
which leads me to ponder the state
of society – so lost in idolatry
always confusing the bible's validity
with false prophecies
all because some can not see
God's world of infinite possibilities
Even though every thing beautiful
around us - came out of His
and then our intangible dreams

THE CHANGE

In September
they Fall
wrapped in shadows
to a un-describable place
all the while
expressing shades of emotions
in yellow, orange
and passionate fiery - reds
crying silently as they wave adieu
still yearning for tomorrow
and the green of one more day

BLATANT POETRY

THE INTRUDER

He wanted her
quiet
He wanted her
to feel his
strong rough hands
plying her long brown legs
a   part
like a little boy
tearing off butterfly wings
in the summer time
EASY
He wanted her to hear
the sound of his zipper
unzipping
SLOW
He wanted her to see him
longing to be inside of her
cutting through her flesh
like butter
He wanted to taste her fear
inhale her anguish – her deep sense of anxiety
He wanted to rock her world to its very core
He wanted to do so many things to her
like tie her up and choke her
call her names like B and WHORE
while making her drop to all fours
just so he could
hypothetically hit it once more
before doing it in reality

THE SURVIVOR

She refused to be
quiet
She hated the feel
of his strong
rough hands
trying to ply her long brown legs
a   part
with the violence of a crowbar
She hated hearing
the sound of his zipper
unzipping - slow
She hated him for
and exposing it to her
all erect and longing to be
inside of her
She despised his anticipation
Her own vivid imagination
for conjuring up images of the violation
of his first thrust inside of her
but most of all
she hated knowing
that he could taste her fear
inhale her anguish – and her deep sense
of anxiety
He was shattering her world
trying to use his power
to dominate her – violate her
and take away her
sacred virginity
by tying her up
and suffocating her
slow
by calling her a B ...
and then a WHORE

before forcing her
to drop to all fours
just so he could
hypothetically
hit it once more
before the cops came

Thank God
the cops came

EGO

Go on
tell yourself
its okay to be
a little bit SELF ISH

After all
you've been doing it
my entire life

BOYCOTTING THE GOING AWAY PARTY

I wanted to forget her
to speed up the process
to bypass the days
the moment
she would be leaving
packing her bags
without a proper goodbye
still disappointed in me
for not being able to
say goodbye
and attend her
going away party
her barbeque
And I know it was selfish of me
but I just wanted to remember
US
the way we were
the way we used to be
truly best-friends
instead of familiar strangers
pretending to be something
that we are not now
and we haven't been
for a such a long time

c l o s e

COMING HOME FROM MONTREAL

Last week
I came home
from Montreal
unpacked my bags
unpacked my worries
avoided my lack of finances
and listened to all the messages
that everyone had left me
while I was gone
and for a moment
I felt special
I felt like the whole world
loved me
like all my dreams
were possible
and everything
was going to be okay
but that feeling
only lasted
a couple of days
and then reality hit me
hard
and I needed my little orange pills
just to make it through
the rigmarole
of my everyday, dead, mortal, state

HYPER-SENSITIVE

Be careful
what you say to me
for my heart is fragile
my mind is deep
and every word
sticks to me
like the pigmentation
of my skin
forging negative alliances
with my soul
where nothing is forgotten
where nothing is lost
because every negative word
replays a thousand times
reverberating in my head
like echoes bouncing off
rugged mountain slopes
and sliding down - sharp
jagged cliffs straight into
a dark never ending abyss
that leaves me filled
with so much rage

THE WHORROR HOUSE

"Shall we turn
a trick for you,
they said
fool you
with our disguise
choke you with
endless flattery
manipulate
your wants
into your most
hated desires
shall we screw u
into the truth
spell reality out
for you real hard
seduce you with your pleasures
while our twisted sisters
chase you
through half open doors
making you forget
that you didn't really
come for us
making you forget
that every "wet dream"
cost you more
more than your willing
to pay for
much more than
you were ever really
ready and able to give
in your misguided quest
to touch and feel God"

THE CYCLE

All day long
they toil
saddled by burdens
no one knows but God
as they raise their children
    sowing seeds
and planting visions and dreams
    for a better life
where the road isn't so rough
and their daughters
don't grow up
bearing their own children
in the midst of adolescence
struggling with all the same
problems they once faced
    when they were
young and restless
and rebelled against
the perfect wisdom of GOD
when He pleaded with them
through their parents voice
PLEASE, my little children
slow down and wait for me
to show you the way - back home

WOUNDED SOULS

PURGING MEMORIES

When you left me
I wrapped up
all of my memories of you
and tossed them
into a big open fire
and watched them burn
burn into ashes
just like my love for you

A BLACK WOMAN FEELING BAD

Black man,
there was a time
I was willing to
serve you
willing to
spend all day
cooking up
curry chicken
with some
rice and peas
blending carrots
in my blender
to squeeze out
carrot juice
laid out
the table
just right for you
light a candle
and waited
and waited
all night for you
It was your Birthday
and I was
so excited
so willing to put you
first
but you never
came home
and I ended up
spending all night
with Billie Holiday
singing and drinking
my blues away
after texting you
21 times

BLUE MOOD

In the night time
I temporarily surrender
To the breaking of my will
wrestling with my
screaming flesh
hungry for its food
and a valid reason why
a substitute for love
is just no good
as the little man
walking on the moon
breaks into my room
plays with my moods
and steals all my words
to my melancholy love song
my melancholy "Blue Mood"

KAMA SUTRA LOVE

You and I
never seem to agree
but I love you anyway
Mr. D ...
I love your
under cover
optimism
your quiet
childish imagination
and the way
you flutter
around our honey moon suite
like a cosmic butterfly
flapping your arms
into wings as you utter
sweet and tender things
and take me in your arms
for the very first time
there - where all senses
      are lost
caught in endless goodbyes
pressed against
your beating chest
that hums the sound of music
to my melancholy heart
ravished by your charms
that hypnotizes
my soul into
following your lead
until we are intertwined
and intoxicated with joy
dripping from each others lips
moon eclipsed with bedroom eyes
taking in nothing more than
our first studio session
co-producing our Kama Sutra love

LIFE GUARD (For OMAR)

I almost
drowned once
when we were little
but you were my Earth
gently pulling me
back to shore

HUMANITY

I work with
deformed limbs
clubbed feet
disabled minds
muted lips
that laugh and smile
with God's humble eyes
underneath
flawed DNA
and stomach tubes
turning fluid from food
into energy for
very special souls

HER WISHES (For Charlene)

She wishes HE could
hear her
She wishes she could
Speak
She wishes she could
get married
She wishes she could
have a baby
She is disabled
and I am able
but she wishes and
    dreams
just like me

TAINTED HISTORY

I've read about
  the Nazis
adding and subtracting
  The Jews
the lifeless bodies
the ink stained
    tattoos
with heads shaven
and minds shell shocked
by unbelievable truths
    and I wonder
    WHAT - WHAT
was the rest of the world doing?

THE INCIDENT

They hang
rustling
outside of my
doorstep
at the very bottom
of the stairs
posted on her mailbox
as unwanted souvenirs
the first a man
made into a skeleton
perched upon a chair
with skin as thin as air
the other
a wheel barrel
full of corpses
piled high like kindling
ready for hot flames
concerned about her mental state
I intercept their mail
and stop their bullets
from reaching their intended target
the middle age schizophrenic woman
down my hallway
full of character
apartment
and many hidden
broken
dreams

THE CHARMER

He interrupted
my thoughts
interrupted my
new found
sense of freedom
stepped into
my world
reached out
his hand
caressed my face
uttered
a few soft spoken
words
smiled so sweet
filled my space
with his presence
his essence
then he told me
things he knew
and he did things
only a few men
from my past
have done
he loved me
he opened up
his heart
and loved me
out of my sadness
out of my darkness
until
I could see again
smile again
believe again
that broken dreams
can still come true

before he poisoned my heart
and made me look and feel
like his fool

FATHER FIGUER

Sometimes
when you are not
watching
I watch the way
you look at her
the way you
smile at her
with loving eyes
guiding her footsteps
gently
as they stumble
through the everyday world
and I love you more
for it – for being
so good with her
for making her
your world
where I am an innocent bystander
re-living
my dysfunctional child
hood
wounded by an absentee father
who never got the chance
to know me
who never got the
chance to be
my first true love

SHE IS YOUR DAUGHTER

At night you watch her sleep
and take comfort
in the whispering wind
that is her breath
Softly you stroke her little hand
That has curled into a tiny fist
and sporadically pulsates
like a heartbeat
in your hand
She is your world
your infinite Universe
filled with endless possibilities
and her 52 smiles
are all the colors in your sunrise
at Dawn
You've loved her since conception
cradled her prematurely at birth
wiping away all of her tears
and yours
when you first
introduced her to the world
as Shambe
a river that flows into an endless ocean
filled with love, life, and beauty
the most powerful part of your legacy
Because she is your daughter
And you are her father
A love so deep at times
it overwhelms your soul
Drying up your throat and making it
hard to swallow
one day
one hour
one minute without her
in your arms

TRUE LOVE

You love
my nuts
and bolts
my screws
and springs
you seem
to love
my everything
and I can't help
but fall apart
around you
and show you
my closet full
of skeletons
and share my memories
filled with demons

EVOLUTION

It took
thirty three years
to find my destiny
along rocky roads
sprinkled with my enemies
in search of prosperous lands
with God alone I learned to shed
    my old skin
as I travel with his guidance and pray
 for more strength
inner peace and wisdom
that I almost thought would come to me
when my restless soul longed for
a clue but only found EGOs
hiding and polluting the truth
until He spoke to me
and blessed me with the proof
that like all His children
I am healed, prosperous, blessed, and free
and able to achieve all he shows me
in visions and dreams
in this ever changing world

THE WITCH HUNT

There goes
those beautiful girls
those angelic girls
that had well known names
that had well known faces
now forever frozen in time
like porcelain dolls
placed carefully
on storage shelves
Those girls will never be
seen again
they will never be
admired again
in fact
I can barely even
remember them now
I can barely even
remember
their magnetic smiles
their rosy cheeks
their fire light hair
because
all that is left of them
is the scent of their perfume
lingering - lingering
in the warm misty air
with the smoldering scent
of their bodies burning - burning into ashes
trapped in the eternal pits of Sheol

THE ORANGE LITTLE PILLS

Those
orange little pills
calm the voices
they hush
the monotone man
singing out loud
inside my head
they block out
the demons
parading around my sanity
antagonizing my serenity
trying to pick a fight
with my deep sense of self
they lull the searing sting of betrayal
and leave me docile
I'm so calm now
I float through reality
on a cloud
no longer rattled
by all the little earthquakes
trying to shatter my soul
and send me straight
back into HELL
where they numb my soul
and hold my mind, my emotions, my will
in a space where I no longer
know, see, or recognize myself

WOUNDED SOUL

At night
she lays in bed struggling
with herself
and the darkness
that hovers over her in silence

Trapped in a cycle of broken dreams
her thoughts unfold and implode
into sensory overload
as she hums a melancholy tune to herself

She is lost - lost in a world
of sexual addiction
low self esteem, drugs, and not enough
Divine providence in her life

She is caught - caught in a spiritual war
beyond her wildest imagination
where the truth has become
a painful weapon
that assaults her soul daily
and threatens to use further force
to bring her towards the light
The light and all that is right
beautiful and powerful – the light that
disperses shadows where ungodly voices
whisper her name and causes her
to feel insane for settling for fools gold
instead of reaching out to God and His
army of angels determined to save her
        wounded soul
from turning mortal men into idols
that lead her to abandon her path to
        enlightenment

just to be a part of their world
   turned sideways at God
run by rebels - devoid of morals
and so certain that Jesus will never return
to battle the devil and his demons
preying on the indecisive nature of the human soul

POLAR OPPOSITES

After I got to know you
your soul seemed like
Amsterdam
lost in group orgies
and legalized contraband

And I felt more like New York City
still shocked by 911
and interrogating George Bush
about what really happened
to those buildings
that held so many lives

THE SWINGERS

He said that
he didn't have it in him
to do it
to take her while
her husband watched
sitting on a chair
across the room
excited by her soul
popping and dropping
down into the dark underworld

So he ran without stopping
and showered for hours
like a traumatized rape victim
understanding for the first time
why this angers God

THE BREAKUP

I cherish our last
  moments
kissing your lips
ever so softly
and inhaling your breath
deeply
as I record the way
the corner of your eyes
scrunch together like a purse
and you smile at me
and hold me in your arms
real close
as I tattoo this feeling
in my heart
and dip my soul
in your soul
one last time
before saying
our final goodbyes

THE SLOW WITHDRAWL

My soul screams
from the fear of separation
but the verdict is in
and everything and everyone
including me
has passed judgment

You are a bird
and I am a fish
and my voice seems to disappear
whenever I am with you
and you never seem to sit still
long enough to see me or you clearly

POWER ROLES

I was trying to be
your woman
your girl
your very best friend
but subconsciously
I guess I was trying
to be your daughter
turned into your whore

Cause I never ever
knew my father

THE LESSON

He said
Woman
you must Learn

and six months later
I did

LIVING OUT LOUD

She knew that
there would be
no peace found
down the barrel
of a gun
no peace found
at the bottom
of a cliff
no peace found
wrapped
in a noose
of a rope

He had left her
and that was all
there was to it
She had lost her voice
she had lost her soul
in the meat packing district
at an after hours club
tucked away in a corner
waiting patiently
to be noticed by the world
waiting patiently to scream
and really live out   LOUD

MY MUSE

On Saturday
I shared my feelings
On Sunday
You disappeared
my disposable
beloved
when was
the moment
you stopped
loving me
what was
the hour
you stopped
caring
we used to
have so much
fun together
we use to
devour
each others
lips
our love making
was so passionate
the most
intense
I've ever felt
We were
so interconnected
and our love
was so urgent
and so sure
that it prompted me
to trust you completely
and tell you everything
about me way too soon

now our love
and your lust for me
are in the past - tense
But I still ache for you
like no one else
even though
you are an enigma
and you move
in manipulating ways
like a contortionist
sliding into puzzles
with missing pieces
and becoming a riddle
full of confusing meanings
with feelings
that are always changing
like a hot and cold faucet
in my brain
forcing me to write down
everything that I feel
in x-rated sentences
with explicit words
 that describes
my spirit
my struggle
my shame
you are the bitter —sweet muse
all great poets
artists and musicians
speak of
and your power
moves me
to spoken word

And
I don't even know
your name

MY CHILDREN

My children
laugh
and smile
and take risks
all the time
they love
innocently
live
egotistically
and open themselves
to creativity all the time
they believe
in real super powers
drink from milk bottles
and love to entertain
for hours
as they giggle
at the word silly
go crazy on candy
and take forever
to settle down
they are honest
little people
who are disturbed by evil
and I envy them
for living
so completely in the moment
all the time
at night they struggle
with their sleep
because for them
life is so interesting
and so sweet
my beautiful - beautiful

children
who are conceived
in other people's wombs
you will never know
how much I love you
and how much
you have blessed my world

DEEPER LESSONS

You and I
were two hurting people
who – somehow
learned
to love one another
and even though its over now
you were my deepest lesson
and I'm even wiser for the experience

GUERILLA BOY

He had robbed
killed
tortured
and maimed

He had done everything
they had told him
to do
everything that would
make him into a man
he had done everything
except learn to LOVE

GOSSIP MONGERS

They were like
Anacondas
regurgitating my pain
just so they could
slay my soul
and eat me alive
again and again

FAME

My people
I worry about you
constantly signing
record deals
and selling your souls
to the Devil
one hit record at a time
I worry about
the way you mislead
our children
with every banging beat
and manufactured
bubble gum rhyme

My people
some of you
have traded in your talents
given to you
by the almighty God
for a moment in the spotlight
and a million tainted dollars

My people
You have lost all sense of
community
and you no longer strive for
Holy unity
only the fabulous life of …
so and so and so - my people
you will reap what you sow
in the next generation
that implodes from your
indifference
and lack of responsibility

to the ones you influence
with your love for materialism
because don't you know
that we are
our most precious resource

YOU WILL NOT FIND ME

You will not
find me
"dropping it
like its hot"
in a music video
and although
"I ain't no saint, yo"
You will not
find me
pimpin or prostituting
myself
just to so call
better myself
because
I am worth
more than
the eye can see
I am a priceless gem
an uncut diamond
and although
I'm not
In the mainstream
Yet
you will soon
hear
my poems rockin
the streets
gliding over powerful beats
as I inject substance
into my video poems
and display images
of the simple things
I thank God for -
Oh, just you wait and see
it will all be
undeniably beautiful

BLACK HISTORY

You have become
Hip-Hop culture
currently twisted
into a lie
and lately I am like
Dianna Ross
singing and acting out
Billie Holiday's tragic demise

Everyday I am monogamy
frustrated by
the endless polygamy in your seed
still hoping to see the Gospel
and other books
filled with great men
like Marcus Garvey, Nelson Mandella,
Fredrick Douglas, Malcolm X,
Martin Luther King Jr.,
Reverend Jessie Jackson,
The Jamaican Maroons
and W. E. Dubois
who stood up for what was right
reflected in you

Black man
I am tired of waiting
to begin my life with you
I have dreams of my own
that need tending to
like Sojourner Truth, Rosa Parks
and Harriet Tubman
I have my own legacy
to leave behind
a legacy that has room for you

But your too busy
setting trends - playing uncommon
to those who choose to be common
and fighting with those
you still call your Public enemies
to stop and just be with me and God
even though we are
apart of everything good
that is rooted down deep
in your tree of life

HEALING

I can see the pain welling up
in your eyes and I don't know if you
come to me in peace or come with more lies
because I've seen your intensity
turn into vindictive rage and I have tasted
your venom and felt the damaging
effects of your words ripping through
my chest like hand grenades
You scare me
and I know eventually if I stay to
unravel your mystery - I might be
destroyed in the process
because you hold a sinister secret
that you refuse to share and because
of this you are a chameleon
that is always changing
your shape
your face
your name
your race
out of fear of rejection you scurry away
like a little mouse
you refuse to be examined
you refused to be analyzed from any real point of view
oh, how you have made me cry
trying and trying so desperately to learn you
and teach you something too
But you refuse to learn and you even tried to
take me down with you
and I almost sank into a depression trying
to get over you
So I told a silly lie to escape you
I learned to be as cunning as you
to overcome your fire with fire

and transform into someone new
a new version of my self – secure in my natural element
so that you couldn't kill my spirit and destroy
my self worth
and with just a little bit more time
I will change again into something new
rid myself of your lies and competition
Then, I will be – I will be ... all over you

DREAMING OF YOU

The other night
I dreamt of you
embraced you
in my arms
and saw myself clearly
in a mirror
half dressed
and trying too hard
to conform

CRUSH

Every time
we speak
I split into
a million and one
atoms
wondering if
my interest in you
will eventually
explode
into another
failed experiment
another
broken down
molecule

SUBLIMINAL MESSAGES

Society says
Don't be
Don't be
Don't be
the odd man
the odd woman
the odd child
that stands out
Don't create
anything original
just jump on
the last beat of the last
Hip-Hop or R&B song
that was a Hit
when it first came out
Don't be creative
Don't be innovative
Don't think for yourself
Don't have your own opinions
or a strong sense of self
Don't be a free spirit
a real poet
who cares about
the meaning
behind your words
instead be like
this or that celebrity
or this or that
musician
or top model
strung out on
crystal Meth
this visible
invisible

well known
unknown
human being
Don't be a leader
be follower and don't
have a unique sense
of style instead watch
"What not to wear"
and meditate daily on
People
Vogue
Elle or Star magazine
For advice on what
to model at church
next week
And ladies - sweet ladies
forget about your wisdom
and all the power and beauty
that you might possess
instead focus on
your booty
and those sexy
thighs and hips
don't worry
don't bother
just forget about
your self-respect
and what your really worth
because that really
intimidates little boys
who are really looking
for little girls
Don't be a strong
out spoken
Black
White
Asian

Portorican
Aboriginal
Middle Eastern
Jewish
Metis
Mexican
Spanish ect…ect…ect
woman
And don't admit that
his infidelities
and endless years
of abuse are serious
transgressions
and crimes against
your soul
don't you ever think
of fighting back
or saying enough is enough
don't step into
your Queendom
and prove that you
are not some whore
Don't have the self-esteem
to wait patiently for a real man
that will respect you
and protect you with his life
instead be passive
and never aggressive
and remain silent
instead of living out loud
forget being real for real
or singing songs
that really matter
songs that might inspire
a couple troubled kids
into changing their distorted
perceptions of this

self-serving world
Don't start a revolution
a revolution that will
never be televised
on any major T.V. station
sponsored by lies
and don't ever speak out
against
the war or wars
that are always happening
on the other side of the world
Don't speak out against
The Judicial system
The politicians
or the social system
That has been failing us
for years
Don't speak out
against any of the bullshit
you see, feel, and hear
because life is just too short
to really stop and care
Don't be
Don't be
Don't be
The odd man
The odd woman
The odd child
that stands out
Don't stick to your
vision and compromise
compromise
compromise
compromise
compromise
your standards
your convictions

your voice
your health
your strong sense of self
until you are a graven image
all over the world
and a complete
stranger to God
to God and to
your   self

COURAGE

Carelessly
You jump
over branches
and leap from
tree to tree
never worrying
about falling
as you reach
for your next meal

Oh how amazing you are
little squirrel
and how I wish
I had your courage
to make my next move

SACRIFICE

He said

let me ease
out of my flesh
for you
smear maroon red
blood
across white walls
for you
break open
my soul and die for you

all in the name of love

let me be
let me be
let me be your sacrifice

and for years I told HIM no

THE MASTER OF DECIET

He is a thug
masquerading
around
like a gentleman
with the temper
of an abusive ex-boyfriend
preying on the innocent
destroying homes
and marriages
using his lips full of eloquence
to whisper lies to foolish men
and start world wars

He is not your friend
No, his ways are wicked
more wicked than any body
ever truly wants to believe
because his moves are subtle
and below the surface
of everything we see,
touch, smell, hear, and feel
he is the Devil
and yes, he is real
but don't take my word for it
seek God and he will be revealed

THE ATHEIST

He says
he doesn't believe
in Jesus
He says
He doesn't believe
in God
but every single night
I hear him
intimately with his wife ...
thanking and praising God
still unaware of how present God is in the details
concerning his life

IMMORTAL

Curl your
lovers lips
around my
fragile
tainted soul
and blow
blow lover blow
blow until
all my dead rose petals
have withered away
and drifted off
with Fall
then kiss me in the Winter time
and bring me back to
s

    p

      r

        i

          n

          g

slow - ly resuscitating my spirit
with love's ecstasy
caressing me with your life energy
until all my wounds have healed
and God will – God will
immortalize your soul

MR. OSHAWA

Gone is the witty
banter
that we once shared
Gone is the feeling
of a million
and one butterflies
fluttering around
inside my stomach
when you are really near
something has
fallen off the shelf
and the magic
from our first conversation
has poofed   and   vanished
into cold
thin   white   air

EXPECTATIONS

The Lord is
my sheppard
and I shall
love even if it is not
returned
respect every person
even when they don't
accept their responsibilities
and act more like my enemies
cursing and using me

I shall not want
sex without
meaning
friendship without
loyalty
relationships
without honesty
company that
does not have
a give and take
mentality
or anything else
that disrupts my soul

because I am an heir
to greatness, a princess, a Queen
a strong and firey spirit
sanctified and washed clean
in Jesus's blood
free from pain
and peaceful in my daddy's arms

INTERNET DATING

HE said he wanted
to fling open
Her curtains
He said he wanted to
pull back
her blinds
He said he wanted
To feel the sun burst
 wide open
but he was only
wasting her time
He said he wanted
To explore her
Hard drive
He said he liked
The clicking of her mouse
He said he was challenged
by her hard drive
He said inside her software
felt safe and warm
He said her program
Was so intriguing
He said her graphics
Were so fierce
He said no other model
Even came close to her
But he was only pushing
Her buttons
He was only
Inflating her low self-esteem
and he gave her a virus –
that she couldn't erase
a virus that wouldn't
be cleaned and then be
blocked her from his
friends list and erased
her from his
compaq memories

MS. LUST

She walks and
sells her beauty
in the middle
of the night
she trades her soul
for a couple
dead presidents
and tells herself
that everything
feels alright
and I pray
and I pray
and I pray for her
and find myself
crying inside

Ms. Holiday

I hope you get to Heaven
Ms. Holiday
where you'll no longer have to sing
the Blues
even though your voice was so beautiful
even though you had a special way
of baring your own simple truth

I hope you get to sing with angels
Ms. Holiday
I hope you get to walk down streets of gold
I hope you bathe in milk and honey
I hope that God makes you whole

I hope eternity is full of joy for you
I hope your veins are injected with love
I hope that whatever tormented you on earth
lays condemned and locked outside Heaven's door
gnashing and grinding its teeth
trapped in the pit of HELL

I hope we get to sing together one day Ms. Holiday
With all the singers that we know
Now that I asked for God's anointing
to touch multitudes of souls

HER FIRST TIME

Her first time was up against
a furnace
during a trivial game of
tug o war
Far from picture perfect
Far from all the fairy tales
She read about as a little girl

Her first time was so unexpected
there were no candles
No flowers
No kisses
No first true love
And all she heard was
heavy breathing and the crackling
sound of a wrapper ripping
and then slowly falling to the floor

This was her introduction
her first experience with "making love"
with jittery hands that tugged at her
poke a dot panties followed by
the application of direct and brutal force

I BE SHE

I be she
I be de black obeah woman
I be de big bad dupe gal
I be de big black ugly bird
sitting pon de banana tree
I be she, I be she, I be she
I be de face of desire
I be de big black mystery
I be de face of passion
I be de wild and wicked spirit
hiding inside de flame
I be in every ocean, mon
I even be in de rain
I be she, I be she, I be she
I be de cool running water
I be de strong island breeze
I be de nicest ackee and salt fish
dat you eva did eat
I be de biggest welcome mat
I be come to Jamaica mon
I be soca, reggae, calypso
and dolla wine too
I be Rastafari, Selassi, Bob Marley
Wen mi smoking mi ganga wid you
but I be at church every Sunday morning, mon
hearing de gospel news
slowly turning into a Christian
to save mi and deliva you
I be she, I be she, I be she
Now I be de poor woman, turn rich woman,
and wise woman too
I be a rude boy – de rude gal
from de original Jamacian
bad gal crew

and mi neva forget mi patois
Since mi move a foreign back in 1982
I be she, I be she, I be she
I be de gal breedin de pikini dem
I be de independent woman too
I be de beat inside de reggae
I be she, I be she, I be she
I be a great many tings ...
long before and long after you
I be she, I be she, I be she

LOVED

She will discover him
When she least expects it
She will believe in him
When she has nothing else
She will face him
When she is broken
She will cry for him
and reach for him
When she is really
in need of help
She will search for him
When she is lonely
in John's
in Peter's
in Jason's
in Mike's
in Paul's
She will inhale him
and forget Him
and that
He is the truth
The way
and the life
She will cut Him
and Kick Him
and curse Him
and Bite Him
and stab Him
and cheat Him
and deny Him
not once
but thrice
she will mock Him
and whip Him

and deny
and deny
and deny
that he is right
no matter how much
he holds her in his
infinite arms and rocks her
gently to sleep at night
calming her fears and making
wonderful plans for the rest
of her human and everlasting life

THE FLESH

The Flesh is hungry
and wants
what its wants
it wants to feed
and bleed
and pull apart
at the seams
until its placed
inside the earth
and out of
the sight of day
it wants to sin
against God
and bask in foreplay
come out at night and distort reality
it wants to crawl deep
into the dark and sleep
life away
it wars against the holy spirit
that commands it to conform to God's ways
it wants to do what it wants to do
whenever it wants to
forgetting its creator
and the final cost
it is a hostile thing
that always tortures and breaks my heart

THE GENTLEMAN

Sometimes
He speaks to me
With THUNDER
And commands
my attention
with LIGHTENING
But with my heart
(with my heart)
He is   a l w a y s
a gentleman
softly knocking at my door
asking if He can please come in
and dine with me
and lately I find myself saying YES
... then, hold on

HAUNTED

He
   b
      l
        e
       e
         d
           s
into my writing
Scars my heart
when He's not near
and the sound of His voice
makes your soul tingle
and every song on the radio
holds you hostage
to the fear of losing Him
to the city
to the night
to the noise
through the pain in everyday life

SWEETNESS

They called him
Sweetness
But he was more like
Sour grapes
twisting up my heart
twisting up my head
and setting
my whole world
and my teeth on edge

THE LANGUAGE

She spoke
the language
of rape
understood
its meaning well
connected with its
violence and held
its shame deep within
herself

Too many of her friends
Knew its language
a language
so misunderstood
by the world
even though
its victims
pay and pay and pay
its price
over and over again

THE RESPONSE

What can I say
My daddy knew
What he was doing
When he made me
Tall dark and beautiful
He was kind and blessed me
With an intelligent
    mind
to help him write
and sing his rhymes
spoken across my mind
deep wide and open
like the ocean
that moves and directs
  endless
    waves
towards the shore
and out to sea again
And it was also my daddy
 that blessed me
with these passionate
    emotions
and my own powerful voice
to make them speak
off the page
in a chorus
that moves
and helps others
bloom with inspiration
from my daddy
  who gives
many gifts
to all the human race
my daddy

who is not
black or white
or Asian
but a mysterious
presence
overflowing
with awesome
spiritual influence
who fills my soul
with elation
and transforms me
this broken
   woman
this once wounded soul
from darkness
   into light
beyond
the grave
after so many
scary nights
that leads me
free to say to you
who shoves
your responsibility
for losing
self-control
my way
No, thanks man
I've got my own
burdens
of responsibilities
to bear and therefore
my own reasons
to care about becoming
better with change
but because
I also care for you

I will tell you
The honest truth
with love
that although
I have this power
You speak so
bitterly of
this power to make
you lose your head
and go crazy
in the flesh
I no longer
can use this power
for evil
Cause, my daddy
has made me
a Queen
who only uses
her powers and skills
to increase His glorious kingdom
and not to send
you on trip
back and forth
to HELL

WISE

He was only
Ten years old
But wise enough
To see
through an episode of
Tom & Jerry
that the wicked never
prosper long
and the righteous
Always inherit the earth
with everlasting abundance
from their consistent
Faith and obedience
to God's Holy son

SUMMER RAIN

It rained a lot last summer
From April, May, June, until July
spontaneously
"pitter pattering"
on my heart like the sound
of a beating drum wooing me
out of my shelter to dance until
I am soaked to the bone with love
And find myself speaking in tongues
wildly excited by your lightening
      CRASHES
And the thunder of your boots
 making their way to me
     unexpectedly
during a warm sunny afternoon
Oh how my soul loves you
As my flesh falls apart around you
   losing its power to move me
out of the reality of your grace
That never deserts me when I am struggling
because you don't need to strike me
in order to show me – who you really are
and that you will always give me your love

SHINE

Wanting to shine
needing to shine
She yearned for a heart
filled with the light
But found
she was allergic
to facing the truth
that she claimed
she longed to find

TIME OF PEACE

Warrior's mask
No longer on display
She wraps the truth
around her waist
and anoints her mind
with silence
as peace spins
on rotation
in and out of
life's living room
joyfully entertaining
God's grace within her salvation

RE-BORN

You
smiling
up at gods
and cursing
God (behind you)

had no clue
did you

that she
a simpleton
liked by few
and judged by
all
for being
tied
to you
and all strung   out
no longer
Be   longs
to you

you

who can never
be

re-born

FAVOUR

In a dream
Evil clearly stands
before me
with explicit eyes
teeth gnashing
fangs and claws gnawing
longing to tear me apart
but in the light of day
God brushes it
all away
and slowly unchains my heart

STRIP TEASE

I want you to
take off your mask
so I can take off mine
I want you to
open your soul
so I can flip through
the pages of your mind
I want you to
look past my luster
and discover
what really makes me
shine
I want you to
stop driving the car
and get in the back seat with me
for just a little while
come on baby,
let God's love be our driver
and let wisdom
open your eyes
to seeing me
for the very first time

SAVIOUR

She was seventeen
With a strong rebellious
    Streak
But even she marveled
At the thought
of Him sitting on His throne
and then stepping done
to die on a cross
just for her

SONGS

M U S I C K - A universal instrument created by God for His praise and worship that is soothing to the soul and has the power to lift evil spirit s away from the sick at heart.

It's lyrics and music can also be used as a destructive force that renders us foolish, when it comes to brainwashing melodies that influence our deep inner thoughts with negative imaginations that lead to sinful choices. Therefore, because music can travel and spread like an ill-fated disease, it is a powerful gift to be used like all powerful gifts on earth … wisely.

SONGWRITING

I never met my biological father but the little I know about him, I hold on to like precious gems. I am told he is a dreamer and a musician, and that I have his bottom lip. I am told that he is tall, slim, light skinned, and very handsome and that he is also a very kind and generous man. This leads me to believe that if we had been given the opportunity to know one another, he would have been my first love and one of my very best friends. Perhaps, that's why although initially I was surprised to discover my ability to write songs and also sing them, I guess I've always known that music was in my blood. Knowing that makes me feel really close to him, and like wherever he is when I get inspired to write a song, sing it, and co-produce it … our souls are united as one.

DREAMS

"Tired" was my very first song. It came to me in a dream. In the dream, I was on a stage standing under a spotlight with Alicia Keys over looking a bunch of empty seats. I remember Alicia Keys telling me to sing and me telling her that I could not, out of fear. Then, she asked me if I could sing, what would I sing? I said I couldn't sing and then I remember opening my mouth and singing "Tired" before waking up and writing down every single word of what would be, my very first song. The next day I told a couple people, including a local vocalist about it, and a couple weeks later it was recorded by her and it has been touching people's souls ever since.

Now push rewind back to five years ago, where I am sitting in an empty bathtub, pregnant, next to a bus shack in Osborne Village with Erykah Badu acting as my midwife. In this dream, Erykah is urging me to give birth to my unborn child but I keep starring at the huge spaceship hovering over me. Until, I find myself hovering under a table with a band-aid on my forehead, across the street, at a Second Cup, waiting for the space ship to do its worst. I remember waking up and feeling like that dream had a special meaning but it would not be years before I figured out what God was trying to tell me about my hidden gifts.

SINGING

I was still in my twenties when I had those dreams, completely unaware of my ability to write songs or my desire to sing them. Therefore, I never imagined that I would not be like all songwriters in the music business, content with the possibility of big royalty checks, and credits given on the inside of album covers people rarely ever read, because they associate the ownership of the song with the singer they idolized on stage. No, I was different. I was like most authors that appreciated the recognition they received after many years of hard work. Therefore, I was not happy with being deliberately pushed into the shadows, so that someone else could "shine". Furthermore, I didn't understand why the songwriter, singer, and the producer couldn't all shine at the same time. After all, no one seem to have a problem with Puffy , The Neptunes, and Timberland producing their beats and receiving as much recognition for their striking beats, as the vocalist that sang on their tracks. I thought about this deeply, after tasting the bitter sting of betrayal every time the singer and producer received recognition for my songs and my name was no where in sight. And after much deep introspection and prayer I realized that receiving royalties and having credit on the inside of an album cover, didn't really cut it for me. I wanted to sing my songs. I wanted to tell the story behind my songs and make my songs my global ministry for God. I didn't want to be listed as a "smorgasborg of writers" on some artist's album. I wanted to sing with every thing in me and pour my heart and soul into each and everyone of my songs. I also wanted to perform my brand of spoken word and inspire others to change their lives for the better. I wanted to express my own experiences in various ways and enjoy God's blessing of recognition for my hard work. I would not be a ghost writer, after all I was also born to let God's light shine through me. I was not born to be silent. I was born to live, speak, and sing the truth and I would own the masters to my songs, and direct the production, promotion, and distribution of my songs. I would train my own voice and pray for God's anointing to sing, and I would not trust my songs to individuals who could not honor my mission/vision to be "a voice for the voiceless" and to inspire others to seek God's will in order to receive positive, social, spiritual, emotional, mental, and physical change.

Well, its been one and a half years riddled with self-doubt, praying and gaining encouraging words from close friends, industry people, since I sang and recorded, my first song "Hurry Up" with butterflies in my stomach. It was a very humbling experience but reading about Billie Holiday, who only had an octave to work with but managed to impact the entire world with her unique voice, excellent sense of timing, rhythm, and ability to emote, gives me hope and the utmost faith that through God and more practice I will be a legendary singer/songwriter, poet, spoken word recording artist, writer, film maker, inspirational speaker, social entrepreneur, wife, mother, daughter, sister, friend, and Christian. After all, anything is possible with God holding my hand!

-Ingrid D. Johnson-

IN THE CLOSET PRODUCTIONS

"A voice for the voiceless"

MUSICAL   CATALOGUE

Songs on album "Wounded Soul"
Volumes 1 & 2
and
Debut album "FLO"

TIRED

(Acoustic Version) written by Ingrid D. Johnson
© 2005 inspired by a dream of Alicia Keys)

Verse 1:   She was tired of being so lonely
           She was tired of sleeping alone
           She was tired of being his baby
           She was tired of waiting at home

CHORUS: She wanted a man
              that she could love
              a real good man
              who loves like God
              like his son …
              like his son …
              like his son …
              like his son …

           Ohhhhhh ….

Verse 2:   Everyday she got up feeling hungry
           She felt hungry for someone to love
           in her heart she wanted a baby
           in her heart she wanted a home

Bridge: As the years went by
          She'd cry and cry
          She'd ask herself
          Oh why can't I
          Find true love
          Find true love
          Find true love
          Find true love

CHORUS

Verse 3: She was tired of being so lonely
She was tired of sleeping alone
She was tired of being his baby
She was tired of being his …
whore

"ALRIGHT"

written by Ingrid D. Johnson © 2005

Verse 1: She was tired, so tired, so tired
of being so lonely
She was tired, so tired, so tired
of sleeping alone
She was TIRED, so TIRED
of being his baby
She was tired, so tired, so tired
of waiting at home

Chorus: It's alright, It's okay
it's alright, it's alright
it's okay
it's alright, it's okay,
it's alright, it's alright,
it's okay

Verse 2: Everyday, everyday, everyday
she felt so un happy.
Everyday, everyday, everyday
she prayed for true love.
EVERYDAY, Everyday
she longed for a baby.
Everyday, everyday, everyday
she longed for a home.

Chorus: It's alright, it's okay
it's alright, it's alright
it's okay
it's alright, it's okay,
it's alright, it's alright,
it's okay

Bridge: Close my door (close my door)
leave your keys
Cause, your words don't mean nothing to me
I was blind (I was blind)
now I see, all the times you were cheating on me

Verse 3:   Tell me Lord, tell me Lord, tell me Lord
why doesn't he love me?
Tell me Lord, tell me Lord, tell me Lord
why love never stays?
Tell me Lord, TELL ME LORD
why am I so lonely?
Tell me Lord, tell me Lord, tell me Lord
why I feel this way?

Chorus: It's alright, it's okay
it's alright, it's alright
it's okay
it's alright, it's okay,
it's alright, it's alright,
it's okay
Pack your bags and just leave
I know someone is out there for me
I'm so glad that I'm free
I'll be fine, so don't worry 'bout me

It's alright, it's okay (**repeat 3 x's then fade**)
it's alright, it's alright,
it's okay

MUSIQ

(written by Ingrid D. Johnson © 2005)

Intro: Music   (spell M.U.S.I.C.)
Sweet, sweet, sweet
Music ... (MUSIC)

Verse 1:   Everyday I wake up
Pray to God
For some love
Look towards His open sky
Til, I hear His voice inside
saying, "life will get a lot sweeter
once I learn to trust Him better".
So, everyday I let Him train me
Don't want this world to break me

Chorus: Mu ... u ... sic
Mu ... u ... sic
Mu ... u ... sic
Mu ... u ... sic
Mu ... u ... sic
Mu ... u ... sic
Mu ... u ... sic
Mu ... u ... sic

Verse 2:   Everyday I go to work
Pay my bills
and tithe at church
and though I got my 9-5
Got to sing my songs tonight
Music makes me feel much bolder
though time is tapping my shoulder
my soul never feels older
so, I'll finally rise and shine

Chorus: Mu ... u ... sic (Hip - Hop)
            Mu ... u ... sic (Reggae)
            Mu ... u ... sic (Soul)
            Mu ... u ... sic (Gospel)
            Mu ... u ... sic (R&B)
            Mu ... u ... sic (Rock)
            Mu ... u ... sic
            Mu ... u ... sic (Jazz)

BRIDGE: (12 bars Hip-Hop MC)

Verse 3: Got to get up on that stage
          Got to get the crowd engaged
          Come on D. J let me hear you play
          been dreaming 'bout
          this night for days
          And the butterflies won't go away
          So, everybody let me hear you say

Chorus: Mu ... u ... sic (sweet)
            Mu ... u ... sic (sweet)
            Mu ... u ... sic (sweet)
            Mu ... u ... sic (sweet)
            Mu ... u ... sic (sweet)
            Mu ... u ... sic (sweet)
            Mu ... u ... sic (sweet)
            Mu ... u ... sic (sweet)

          (dah, dah, dah, dah, dah)
          (dah, dah, dah, dah, dah)

Chorus: Mu ... u ... sic
           Mu ... u ... sic
           Mu ... u ... sic
           Mu ... u ... sic
           Mu ... u ... sic
           Mu ... u ... sic
           Mu ... u ... sic
           Mu ... u ... sic

Outro:

Martin Luther King Jr.
"Had a dream"
and with Obama it finally came true
So, if you have a dream
make sure you go out there
And let God make it come true for you
and don't forget to support other peoples's dreams too.

"I BELIEVED"

(written by Ingrid D. Johnson © 2005)

Verse 1:   Boy, I heard you
on the phone
you thought
You were alone
when you said
You loved her
Now I'm hurting inside
so tired of your lies
How could you
Cheat on me with her

Chorus: I believed, I believed
When you said,
Baby trust me
I believed, I believed
When you told me not to worry
I believed, I believed
That we were truly happy
Now I'm losing my mind
thinking 'bout those times
you said you were at work

Verse 2:   Boy, what you did
was cruel
you thought I was
your fool
But, I heard everything
you said
You were making future plans
and telling all your friends
you didn't love me anymore

Chorus: I believed, I believed
When you said,
Baby trust me
I believed, I believed
When you told me not to worry
I believed, I believed
That we were truly happy
Now I'm losing my mind
thinking 'bout those times
you barely even touched me

(Musical Solo)

Verse 3:   How could you
treat me so bad
you make me
so mad
But, one day
it'll be your turn
You'll let down
your guard
love with all your heart
and that woman
will betray you

Chorus: I believed, I believed,
That you would always love me
I believed, I believed,
That we were truly happy
I believed, I believed
someday that we'd get married
Now, I'm losing my mind
thinking 'bout those times
you barely even touched me

I believed, I believed,
When you said,
Baby trust me
I believed, I believed
When you told me not to worry

I believed, I believed
That we were truly happy
I'm losing my mind
thinking 'bout those times
you barely even touched me

(Repeat last chorus 3 times)

"FLO-ING ENERGY"

written by Ingrid D. Johnson & Florence Oramasionwu © 2006

INTRO: (4 bars)

what you do to me ... is undeniably... sweet ecstasy
... what ... you ... do ... to ... me

Ingrid: what you do to me ... fill me up with ecstasy ...
Boy, you don't know what you do to me ...

CHORUS: (8 bars)
I need to be with you
I long to be with you
you satisfy my needs
and complete my dreams
I need to be with you
I long to be with you
you're my destiny
your love is ecstasy

VS.1   (16 bars spoken word)
There's been something
I've been wanting to tell you
for quiet a long time – something
that runs and skips across my mind
(daily ... echo 3 times)
Whenever I'm in your arms
life seems so beautiful and full of joy
Before I met you
I was dying inside
But your love cured my disease
now I'm high on life
and I can't imagine my world
without you in it
When you're not near

I feel so empty – that's how I know
that you're my (destiny … echo 3 times)
So, please baby … don't ever leave me

CHORUS: (8 bars)
I need to be with you
I long to be with you
you satisfy my needs
and complete my dreams
I need to be with you
I long to be with you
you're my destiny
you're love is ecstasy

VS.2 (Flo 16 bars)

There's something
'bout your presence
its in your very essence
can't take my eyes off of you
when you walk in a room
you've got my full attention
fill me with anticipation
I crave to be near you
want to be around you
can't communicate
the feelings you create
no more worries or fears
they disappear when your near
you peak all of my senses
and break down my defenses
send tingles up and down my spine
you do it every time

CHORUS: (8 bars)
I need to be with you
I long to be with you
you satisfy my needs

and complete my dreams
I need to be with you
I long to be with you
you're my destiny
you're love is ecstasy

Vs.3   (16 bars)

(Flo)   When I saw you from the start
(Ing)   Boy, you were such a beautiful work of art
(Flo)   you're energy draws me
(Ing)   your soul has captured my heart
(Flo)   you love me inside out
(Ing)   that's why, my love, you are my muse
(Flo)   your touch ripples through my body
(Ing)   as you inspire me
(Flo)   to sing sweet harmonies
(Ing)   and to write lines upon lines of poetry
(Flo)   you teach me
(Ing)   and your kiss transforms me
(Flo)   you help me shed my layers
(Ing)   from a caterpillar into a butterfly
(Flo)   your love propels me
(Ing)   and makes me rise into eternity

CHORUS: (8 bars)
                I need to be with you
                I long to be with you
                you satisfy my needs
                and complete my dreams
                I need to be with you
                I long to be with you
                you're my destiny
                you're love is ecstasy (repeat twice)

"MY SOUL"

(written by Ingrid D. Johnson © June 2006)

Verse 1: (8 bars)
Lately … been dreaming 'bout you, baby
I know this all sounds … crazy
but, your spirit is amazing
and, I don't wanna … wreck things
So, I won't say… nothing
Cause, you are my … best friend
And I put that on everything

Chorus: (4 bars)
My soul – my soul
My soul won't let you go
my soul – my soul
My soul won't let you go

Verse 2: (8 bars)
Yesterday, we were chilling
and you caressed my face
then you said in a playful way
that you and I were soul mates
and my heart just skipped a beat
I could feel your love all through me
So, I said I just got to leave
but you refused to just let me be

Chorus: (4 bars)
My soul – my soul
My soul won't let you go
my soul – my soul
My soul won't let you go

Bridge: (12 bars) Hip-Hop MC NDU

Verse 3: (8 bars)
By my door is where you
opened up and let me know
All the feelings you had never shown
So, when you touched me I just let it go
All the things that you didn't know
I said I loved you and you echoed
You kiss my lips and I felt ecstasy
Your love is heaven and I'm finally free

Chorus: (4 bars)
My soul – my soul
My soul won't let you go
my soul – my soul
My soul won't let you go   (Repeat 2 times)

"MOVE ON"

(by Ingrid D. Johnson, & Florence Oramasionwu © 2006)

Verse 1: There were so many roads
I didn't know which way to turn
Then I heard my conscious say
to take this road and don't you worry
although the path is rough
you'll find your way through life's journey
then a doubtful voice told me
to take the simple road and go easy

(Pre-chorus) But I know that everything will be alright
Cause, I know there'll be a better day
All I gotta do is keep on holding tight
Keep the faith and things will come my way (way)

(Move on, Move on, Move on)

Chorus: Everything's been said and done
time to take your dreams and run
but just something keeps telling me

(move on, move on, move on)

He whispers in my ear
Drop those worries and those fears
Girl you know your ready
just move on, be strong

Verse 2: There alone all by myself
I tossed and turned inside my head
Then with my two eyes closed
I chose a path my soul felt most

then I heard my thoughts scream out to me
wait your not ready yet
but I chose to trust myself
ignore my fears and walk ahead

(Pre-chorus)   But I know that everything will be alright
Cause, I know there'll be a better day
All I gotta do is keep on holding tight
Keep the faith and things will come my way (way)

(Move on, Move on, Move on)

Chorus: Everything's been said and done
time to take your dreams and run
but just something keeps telling me
move on, move on,

He whispers in my ear
Drop those worries and those fears
Girl you know your ready
just move on, be strong

Bridge: Life's too short
to sit around and wait
for things to happen,
so take life by the hand
and follow - follow your dreams (repeat 2xs)
follow - follow destiny

"ONLY YOU"

(by Ingrid D.Johnson, & Florence Oramasionwu © 2006)

CHORUS: I close my eyes at night
and dream of you
through open fields
bare feet I run to you
like an untamed flame
my soul - my soul it craves
for you ... and only you

Verse 1: You're in my heart   Female
You're in my mind
Your touch is with me
All the time

Seven years I've wasted here   Male
Do anything to get you near   Male and Female
I'm so in love with you
I've cried these tears
A lifetime I'll wait for you   Female
wish you were here

CHORUS: I close my eyes at night
and dream of you
through open fields
bare feet I run to you
like an untamed flame
my soul - my soul it craves
for you ... only you

Verse 2: Late at night I watch you sleep   Male
I whisper to you in your dreams
Late at night wrapped in my dreams   Female
I feel your love surrounding me

Why did you leave me   Male and Female

I feel so alone   Female
life is so empty
here on my own

CHORUS: I close my eyes at night
and dream of you
through open fields
bare feet I run to you
like an untamed flame
my soul - my soul it craves
for you ... only you

BRIDGE: I close my eyes and
see the rainfall –fall
right down my eyes
we walk like shadows
I try to follow
and fall - fall a step behind

CHORUS: I close my eyes at night
and dream of you
through open fields
bare feet I run to you
like an untamed flame
my soul - my soul it craves
for you ... only you

"NOT TOO LATE"

(written by Ingrid D. Johnson © 2006)

VERSE 1:   On a summers day
I was walking through the park
when I saw your face
and felt something just break my heart.
Then I felt your hands
wrap slowly round my waist
and I heard your voice
say, girl its not too late (too late, too late)

CHORUS: Not too late for loving
Not to late for something
Not too late for anything
worth having (yeah, yeah, yeah) (repeat 2xs)

VERSE 2:   On a cloud in my dreams
you were standing next to me
and I could hear you breath
and feel your soul just haunting me
so many memories
my heart kept telling me
He's the man of your dreams
so girl just go and get him

CHORUS: Not too late for loving
Not to late for something
Not too late for anything
worth having (yeah, yeah, yeah) (repeat 2xS)

BRIDGE: Wish I could tell you
how deep my love is
how I think of you baby
and long for you still.

VERSE 3:   Woke up out of my sleep
and you weren't lying next me
and I felt so empty - my soul
just kept on screaming
It was a tragedy, drowning in those memories
of what could've have been, if only I were happy
But I was incomplete, so when you came back
looking for me, so I was not ready and broke your heart
on July. 13th, 13th, 13th, (echo)

CHORUS: Not too late for loving
Not to late for something
Not too late for anything
worth having (yeah, yeah, yeah)
(repeat 3x's times and fade…)

"YOUR SMILE"

(written by Ingrid D. Johnson copyright 2007)

INTRO: Back- back– back in the day
Back-back-back in the day
Back – back in the day

Verse1:   She was nine years old
when he stole her soul
and he destroyed her home
and he left her all alone
So filled with pain - she felt
so ashamed - she lived in chains
and nearly went insane

Chorus: I see the tears that you cry
I see the pain in your smile
your smile, your smile, your smile …
your smile, your smile, your smile …

Verse2:   Burned again
by lovers flames
so drawn to pain
she gives herself away
hoping he would be
everything she dreamed
but in reality - he's nothing like he seems
Wondering when
time will mend
the things they did and all the pain she feels
its so intense - she tries to end
a life she's spent trying not to feel

Chorus: I see the tears that you cry
I see the pain in your smile

your smile, your smile, your smile …
your smile, your smile, your smile …

BRIDGE: Little girl don't you know
That your second to none
So be a Queen and stand
Stand on your own
Although your mommy
and daddy have left you alone
the Lord is good and will give you
a home of your own

CHORUS: He sees the tears that she cries
He sees the pain in her smile
her smile, her smile, her smile …
her smile, her smile, your smile …

Verse 3: In her book - they take a look
And feel so shook
from all the things she says
two men did - when she was a kid
without a clue - who to turn to
Older now – she shouts it out
With nothing left – nothing left to lose

CHORUS: Till, He sees the tears that she cries
He sees the pain in her smile
her smile, her smile, her smile …
her smile, her smile, your smile …

"NO MORE"

(Written by Ingrid D. Johnson copyright 2006)

INTRO: Female MC

VS:1 I heard the news today
that you were leaving me
and I don't know what to say
except I love you B
and I wish that you could see
that we were meant to be
and put some faith in me
and our family
you say the spark is gone
from this relationship
and things are way to hard
and you can't handle it

CHORUS: So, you gotta go
you gotta leave
Gotta turn your back
say goodbye to our kids
no more mommy and dad
no more mommy and dad

Vs:2 Now everyday at work
my thoughts are on you B
and how much it hurts
without you next to me
you broke our children's hearts
since you went away from me
and life is really hard
and I don't get much sleep
I'm wondering where you are
and if you are happy
just lying in his arms
and always haunting me

CHORUS: cause , you had to go
you had to leave
you had to turn your back
say goodbye to our kids
no more mommy and dad
no more mommy and dad

Bridge: 12 bars FEMALE MC

Vs3: Now, twenty years are gone
and our girls are all grown up
driving daddy's car
and winning scholarships
still wondering where you are
and why you gave them up
and never ever called
to see the scars you left
deep within their hearts
cause you couldn't handle it
and never did your part
and missed out on their firsts

CHORUS: Their first step
Their first kiss
their first love, yeah
where were you
too bad Boo
when they wanted your love
when they needed your love (yeah)

"LET IT GO"

Written by Ingrid D. Johnson copyright 2007

INTRO: (Music)

Vs1: Spent her life
living out a boxes
in hotel rooms
trying to make a profit
on her back
cause no one ever noticed
her pain inside
or the pictures in her locket

pre-chorus: Little girl you know
you must find a way to
find a way
to escape the pain
and all the things
that blinds you

Go, let it go
let it go
let it go
let it go now

Vs2: Hiding from
the man inside her closet
filled with rage
he takes her
for his hostage
on her face
so many bruises
the price she pays
for avoiding kisses

pre-chorus: See the beauty
in your face
forget the things
time will erase
forget the past
and your mistakes
and just let it

Go, let it go
let it go
let it go
let it go now

Musical SOLO

Vs.3 Eighteen years
She tried so hard
to please her
filled with tears
cause she couldn't
reach her
hurt inside
cause she disowned her
left to find
another to call mother

CHORUS: Go, let it go
let it go
let it go
let it go now (repeat 3xs and fade)

"HURRY UP"

created by Ingrid D. Johnson copyright 2007
(Part of intro inspired by Florence Oramasionwu)

INTRO: So long for my / puzzle piece
So long for my / lock and key
So long for my / dreams to be
I've been waiting / for that man
that's meant for me

Verse 1: Everyday I - Every day I - Everyday I
Everyday I sit and pray for
my dreams to come true
wondering when I'll
see your face boy
I'm missing you

CHORUS: Hurry up
Hurry up
and get here boy
Hurry up
Hurry up
and hold me in your arms
Hurry up
Hurry up
I need you now
Hurry up
Hurry up
I just can't wait no more

Verse 2: Alone at night I
close my eyes and
dream about you
we've never met boy
but I just know that
I was meant for you

And every time
I think I'm okay
and fine without you
my soul just shakes
and my body aches
and I long for you

CHORUS: Hurry up
Hurry up
and get here boy
Hurry up
Hurry up
and hold me in your arms
Hurry up
Hurry up
I need you now
Hurry up
Hurry up
I just can't wait no more

BRIDGE: I wrote this song for you
Feel so much for you
want to say I do
I do, I do, I do
love you   (repeat 2xs)

Verse 3: Come to my window
and see the candle
burning for you
please don't be shy boy
give love a try boy
and make our dreams come true
It took some time but
Now I know that
I'm ready for you
So, if you want me
Come and find me

And all this love for you
Yes, all my love's for you.

CHORUS: Hurry up
Hurry up
and get here boy
Hurry up
Hurry up
and hold me in your arms
Hurry up
Hurry up
I need you now
Hurry up
Hurry up
I just can't wait no more.

"Gonna Treat U"

(Interlude) lyrics and melody by Ingrid D. Johnson

Gonna treat you nice today
Gonna treat you kind today
No matter how I feel today
Gonna show you love today

I think about you every day
And even if you will not stay
I'll get down on my knees and pray
Praise God for you.

FEEL THE WAY I FEEL

(copyright 2007 by Ingrid D. Johnson)

Verse 1: Boy ... I'm finally ready
I mean really ready and open
after chilling with Sofia (God's daughter)
wisdom for such a long time
after spending a year in Heaven
on earth and like Maya Angelou's
love poem from Medea's family reunion
traveling "in and out" ..."in and out" of time

Chorus: You turn me in
You turn me out
and in your arms
I feel His love
and every time I feel you near
my fears and doubts disappear (yeah ...)
Tell me ... do you feel the way I feel
Cause, I need to know this things for real

Verse 2: At the beginning of our journey
He the glorious one took me
Soul searching on planets and deep
into atmosphere's I never really knew
where He slowly broke down
all the soul ties with ex- lovers
I once tried so hard to hold on to
Ties that kept me from really seeing
me or even seeing you
ties that kept me from really loving myself
loving Him and loving you
and I was grateful ... so grateful

Chorus: You turn me in
You turn me out
and in your arms
I feel His love
and every time I feel you near
my fears and doubts just disappear (yeah ...)
please tell me ... do you feel the way I feel
sweet baby, please say your love's for real

Verse 3: And at the end our journey
Sweet Adam my soul mate
My husband – my prince
He gave me a gift so sweet
and so true that tasted like honey
which warmed my heart
opened up my soul
and left me filled with visions
sweet visions and dreams of me and you
that felt strange at first but slowly
everyday made "us" brand new
Oh, Adam, he restoreth our souls
and our cups runneth over
surely His goodness mercy and kindness
shall follow us all the days of our lives
and we shall dwell in the house of
the lord   forever

CHORUS: Chorus: You turn me in
You turn me out
and in your arms
I feel His love
and every time I feel you near
my fears and doubts disappear (yeah ...)
Tell me ... do you feel the way I feel
Sweet baby , know this love's for real
Know this love's for real

(I know, I know, I know, I know ...)

"I DON'T CARE"

(copyright 2007 by Ingrid D. Johnson & Florence Oramasionwu)

Intro: When I was young I was wild
When I was young I was wiiiiiild

Verse: 1 When I was young
I was wild
and you use to say
some ugly things
all the time
never thinking
I was struggling
I was struggling
Till you heard from a girl
on the other side of the world
'bout my books and all my beautiful words
(my beautiful words)

CHORUS: I don't Care
If you don't believe in my dreams
gonna fly
gonna fly
and do so many things
(do so many things)-

Verse 2: Was the girl
on the outside
always looking in
trying to find just a way
to make it all begin
make it all begin
had this dream
no one wanted to believe
in my voice or my choice
to make this destiny
make this destiny

CHORUS: I don't Care
                If you don't believe in my dreams
                gonna fly
                gonna fly
                and do so many things –
                do so many things – (repeat 2xs

Verse 3:   Had the style
                Had the moves
                and all the wonderful grooves
                Had the steps
                and the grace
                To take the first place
                To take the first place
                Felt the beat
                Had the heat
                To make my body speak
                walk through the door
                and I can hear
                the crowd roar
                ENCORE

CHORUS: I don't Care
                If you don't believe in my dreams
                gonna fly
                gonna fly
                and do so many things
                (do so many things)- (repeat 3xs)

"LOVE YOU BABY"

Copyright 2008 Ingrid D. Johnson

VERSE 1: Baby …
I'm so into you
what else can a sistah do
But tell you how I feel today
and hope you feel
The same old way

CHORUS: Oooooh, oh, oooooh …
how I love, how I love,
how I love you baby
Boy, you drive me crazy
Oooooh, oh, oooooh …
how I wish, how I wish,
I could be your lady
and have your babies

VERSE: Spending hours
on the phone
You tell me things
nobody knows
and in my heart
this love thing grows
So baby I was wondering
if this girl who's been your friend
can be your woman til the end.

CHORUS: Oooooh, oh, oooooh …
how I love, how I love,
how I love you baby
Boy, you drive me crazy
Oooooh, oh, oooooh …
how I wish, how I wish,

I could be your lady
and have your babies

BRIDGE: (12 bars MC)

VERSE 3:   I know you think
She's pretty fine
and maybe
she will treat you kind
but she'll never
love you
more than me
Cause, you and I
were meant to be
so I'll wait until you see the truth
cause, Heaven knows I'm digging you
so I'll cry and pray to God for you - for you

CHORUS: Oooooh, oh, oooooh …
how I love, how I love,
how I love you baby
Boy, you drive me crazy
Oooooh, oh, oooooh …
How I wish, How I wish, I could be
your lady
but I know you'll play me.

"WANTING TO LOVE YOU"

INTRO: Baby
Baby, Baby
I'm in
I'm in love with you
Baby
Can't you
See I
See I love you

(musical solo 4 bars)

CHORUS: Wanting to love you
Wishing I could touch you
Place no one above you
Except, God who loves you
(who loves you, who loves you) 1x

VERSE 1:   I pass you by
and close my eyes
and want to cry … yyy
Cause, your cold as ice
And you don't look twice
And I'm too shy … yyy
to ask you why
you never smile
when I am walking by yyy
you make me cry and boy
that's no lie
When will you see me …

CHORUS: Wanting to love you
Wishing I could touch you
Place no one above you

Except, God who loves you
(who loves you, who loves you) (repeat 2xs)

VERSE 2:   Late at night
When the moon is bright
I fall asleep
and dream you
I don't know why
you touch my life
so I can't help but breath you
til you move in me
and I'm set free
basking in your presence

BRIDGE: Please don't
go a way from me
Cause, I can't bear it
If you leave
So, say you love me
Or set me free
Say you need me
Or just let me be

CHORUS: Wanting to love you
Wishing I could touch you
Place no one above you
Except, God who loves you
(who loves you, who loves you)
Wanting to love you
Wishing I could touch you
Place no one above you
Except, God who loves you

Can't you see
I love you

"TIME FOR A CHANGE"

NTRO (MC) 8 bars

VERSE 1:   So much going on
in this world I see
But the government
Won't even talk to me
got so much to say
Wanna speak my piece
and all they ever do
is practice to deceive
'bout the things they do
and the things they've done
after all of this
they still can't help no one

CHORUS: (ahhhh ...)
So, maybe its time
for a change
(ahhhh ...)
time to make
a move or a play
(ahhhh ...)
Yeah, baby
It's time for a change
(ahhhh ...)
together we can find
a new way

VERSE 2:   Life is full of
so many ups and downs
and everybody
Just keeps running 'round
on a mission to

get what's there's
while there brother lives
trapped in despair
'til the genocide is finally done
and the chips are all
scattered on the ground

CHORUS : (ahhhh ...)
So, maybe its time
for a change
(ahhhh ...)
time to make
a move or a play
(ahhhh ...)
Yeah, baby
It's time for a change
(ahhhh ...)
together we can find
a new way

BRIDGE: HIP HP MC (12 bars)

CHORUS: (ahhhhh ...)
Cause, its time for
a change ...
(ahhhh ...)
time to make
a move or a play
(ahhhh ...)
Yes, people it's time
for a change
(ahhhh ...)
we gotta let God
lead the way (repeat 3x)

I said we gotta let God lead the way
Cause, baby its time for a change. (repeat 3xs)

"THINGS YOU DO"

written by Ingrid D. Johnson copyright 2007

CHORUS: I … (I … I … I …)
Don't wanna hear 'bout
the things you do
with your posse
Cause, I (I…I…I)
always wonder when
you'll quit the crew
and be somebody

VERSE: 1 Boy …
I've always loved you
since little kids rode on horses
And boy …
I always hung on to
your promises
even when you were naughty
Cause, boy
I always wanted to wear your ring
and be your wifey (yes, your wifey)

CHORUS: I … (I … I … I …)
Don't wanna hear 'bout
the things you do
with your posse
Cause, I (I…I…I)
always wonder when
you'll quit the crew
and be somebody

VERSE: 2 Years …
I sat up waiting by the telephone
So afraid that you

would never ever ever
make it home and be killed
Out there …
running 'round with all your little boys
filled with fear, no faith, that God
would ever, ever, make a way

CHORUS: So, I … (I … I … I …)
Don't wanna hear 'bout
the things you do
with your posse
Cause, I (I…I…I)
always wonder when
you'll quit the crew
and be somebody

INTRO: (8 bars MC)

BRIDGE: Gonna have to leave you
baby … (ohhhhh)
It's a shame
Can't wait no more
'til you to get out of the game
And though your special, daddy
(ohhhhh) you're the one to blame
Can't sit around
waiting for you to change

CHORUS: Cause, I … (I … I … I …)
Don't wanna hear 'bout
the things you do
with your posse
Cause, I (I…I…I)
always wonder when
you'll quit the crew
and be somebody (repeat 3xs)

"YOU AND ME"

Copyright 2008 Ingrid D. Johnson

INTRO: La, la,
La, La
La, la, la,
La, la,
La, la, la la, la…

CHORUS: When its You and me
and la, la, la, la, la, la
when its you and me
la, la, la, la … (repeat 1 x)

VERSE 1: I like the way
you hold me
when your happy
and the way you kiss me
softly
and I like the way
you squeeze me
til, I am dizzy
and the way
you move me baby

CHORUS: When its you and me
and la, la, la, la, la, la
when its you and me
la, la, la, …

VERSE 2: And I like the way
you pause when life
gets busy
just to call and say
you miss me

and I like the way
you hurt when I am hurting
and the way
you comfort me

CHORUS: When its You and me
and la, la, la, la, la, la
when its you and me
la, la, la, la, ...

VERSE 3: And I like the way
You never cease
to amaze me
like when we pray
and you thank God for me
and I like the way
you tell me
I'm your family
And the way you say
You complete me

BRIDGE: I love the way
We always grow
your exactly what I need
and I like the way
you take things slow
just to prove your love's
for real
And I love the way
You hold my hand
And support me in my dreams

CHORUS: When its You and me
and la, la, la, la, la, la
when its you and me
la, la, la, ... (repeat 3 times and fade)

"OH, OH "

written by Ingrid D. Johnson 2008

Verse 1:   She cuts and bleeds
wondering when
the pain will end
inside her
And at night she dreams
'bout the man that lurks
behind the shadows
reaching out
to find another

Chorus: OoooooH, OH
OoooooH, OH, OH, OH , OH (repeat 2xs)

Verse2:   He kicks and fights
Every time
they try to love him
and alone he cries
about the man who fail to lead him
who used his fist as way to teach him
and left him in
a world of aggression

Chorus: OoooooH, OH
OoooooH, OH, OH, OH , OH (repeat 2xs)

BRIDGE: And I say how
how can we make it through
if no one will tell us the truth
or show us were loveable
And I say how
How can we learn to dream
If no one will see past our pain
or take time to show us the way

Chorus: OoooooH, OH
OoooooH, OH, OH, OH , OH (repeat 4xs)

"HOW I"

written by Ingrid D. Johnson 2008

Chorus:
How I
wish I
could tell you how my love is
How I
wish I
could show you
how I feel (

Verse 1:
You never ever leave my dreams
Oh, you're my fantasy
And even in reality
baby you know your my destiny
If I can only speak
Maybe you would notice me
up and run away with me
my baby, my baby, my baby

Chorus:
How I
wish I
could tell you how my love is
How I
wish I
could show you
how I feel (

Verse 2:
From the first time
that I saw your face
Man, had to give God the praise
And the first time that I heard you speak
Your wisdom it made my soul weep
And then when you said my name (Ingrid)
My heart exclaimed

can't believe God answered my prayers
my baby, my baby, my baby

BRIDGE :   Ooooooh
come away with me
wrap yourself up in these arms
Yeah, baby can't you see
you don't have to worry
baby let's get married
No more girls will break your heart
Yeah, come and dance with me
you and I we can be free
let my kiss just say it all

Chorus: Nooooow I
wish I - wish I
could tell you how my love is
Noooooow I
know I
could show you
how I my love is -love is

I can show you my love (repeat 7xs and fade)

INGRID D. JOHNSON

Ingrid D. Johnson is a Winnipeg-based published poet, spoken word recording artist, singer-songwriter, producer, social activist, social entrepreneur, inspirational speaker, and Filmmaker.

Johnson wrote songs "Tired", "My Soul", "Alright", "I Believed" and co-wrote "Only You", "Move on", and "Flo-Ing Energy" on R&B vocalist FLO's self-titled debut album "FLO" (also available on CD baby). The album, which received 4 out of 5 stars in The Winnipeg Sun, The Winnipeg Free Press, and Winnipeg's Uptown Magazine listed Johnson's first song "Tired" as being one of the songs on the album that gave the album its diversity. Johnson says the song was inspired by a dream she had of Alicia Keys asking her the question, "if you could sing ... what would you sing?" Her response turned into a boho-jazz creation that expresses the way she felt about intimate relationships at the time.

Johnson's first collection of poetry "Little Black Butterfly in Iridescent Sunlight," deals with the emotional trauma of childhood incest as well as issues with low self-esteem, dysfunctional relationships, lust, love, introspection, and spiritual transcendence. Since the launch of the book, on July.13th 2005, it was number five on the bestseller's list at McNally Robinson. She has received public support and exposure for her work in The Winnipeg Public Library's 2006 September/October newsletter, The Metro and The Lance community paper, and Uptown (local Arts paper). She has been showcased on Def Poetry Jam's website (hosted by Verse Makers), appeared on FLAVA 107.9's Big Phat Morning show, interviewed on CKUW's "Grammar Skool" and "Say it Sistah" radio show on 95.9 F.M., CBC's Radio One "Up to Speed" show, CBC's National radio show "Outfront", CBC local news, CBC News world, Shaw T.V., and Bravo!News (Chum T.V.). In May 2008, Johnson was also featured on Hawaii's internet blog talk radio show "MIC CHECK".

Johnson enjoys using her poetic skills to confront social issues, offer hope, and inspire change. On April.21st 2007, Johnson participated in V-day (Eve Ensler's "Vagina Monologues")to help stop violence against women. Shortly after, she received an invitation to Toronto's 7th Annual Reel World Film Festival & Hawaii's Girl Fest to screen her first short, experimental, narrative " The Real Woman".

Also by Ingrid D. Johnson
courtesy of *In The Closet Productions*

Little Black Butterfly In Iridescent Sunlight

Black Butterfly (Spoken Word CD)

Available for purchase at www.intheclosetproductions.com